NAVIGATION
from Then to Now

BY RACHEL GRACK

AMICUS | AMICUS INK

Sequence is published by Amicus and Amicus Ink
P.O. Box 1329, Mankato, MN 56002
www.amicuspublishing.us

Cataloging-in-Publication Data is available from the Library of Congress.
ISBN 978-1-68151-683-7 (hard cover)
ISBN 978-1-68151-765-0 (eBook)
ISBN 978-1-68152-469-6 (paperback)

Editor: Wendy Dieker
Designer: Aubrey Harper
Photo Researcher: Holly Young

Photo Credits: Lev Dolgachov/Alamy cover; KOHb/iStock cover; LeoPatrizi/iStock 4; jk78/iStock 7; Royal Geographical Society/Getty 8; Valentin Vodnik/WikiCommons 8–9; DR Travel Photo and Video/Shutterstock 10–11; Keystone View/FPG/Getty 12; Andrey Bayda/Dreamstime 14–15; Didier Marti/Getty 16–17; Stefan Sollfors/Alamy 19; franckreporter/iStock 20–21; valentinrussanov/iStock 22–23; Blazej Lyjak/Alamy 24–25; Martyn Goddard/Getty 27; Julia Lavrinenko/Alamy 28–29

Printed in the United States of America

HC 10 9 8 7 6 5 4 3 2 1
PB 10 9 8 7 6 5 4 3 2 1

TABLE OF CONTENTS

Finding Your Way

You want to visit a friend in a nearby city. How do you find your way? That's easy! Type the address into a **smartphone** and follow the directions. But long ago, people had to find other ways to **navigate**. Imagine no highways or street signs. No map to read. From ancient times to today, the way we find our way has changed.

A smartphone with a map is handy when traveling to a new city.

The First Maps

Look up! People once used the sun, moon, and stars for directions. The positions of **celestial bodies** helped guide them. Around 150, a Greek **astronomer** named Ptolemy drew maps of the sky. People could follow the sun from east to west. They looked for the North Star at night. They knew which way was north.

The starry sky was once one of the best ways for people to navigate.

Ptolemy's celestial maps guide travelers.

150

. . L O A D I N G . . . L O A D I N G .

Ptolemy's celestial
maps guide travelers.

LOADING... LOADING.

Cartographers in
Rome start drawing
road maps of Europe.

Around 300, **cartographers** in Rome started drawing maps of the land. The maps were kept updated over the years. By 1200, one map showed 60,000 miles (96,560 km) of roads and more than 500 cities! Roads stretched from Western Europe to the Middle East. The map also marked rivers and forests. It even showed where to find temples and spas.

The ancient Roman road map (inset) led to the maps and globes Gerardus Mercator made in the 1500s.

In 1300, a new tool helped travelers. It was a **compass**! A needle inside always pointed north. It used the Earth's **magnetic field** to show directions. Travelers didn't need to see the stars anymore. Rain or shine, day or night, it kept people moving in the right direction.

Since the 1300s, travelers have used compasses to know which way is north.

Ptolemy's celestial maps guide travelers.

The compass becomes a common navigation tool.

150   300   1300

G . . . L O A D I N G .

Cartographers in Rome start drawing road maps of Europe.

Drivers on US Highway 1 check their map. How far to the next turn?

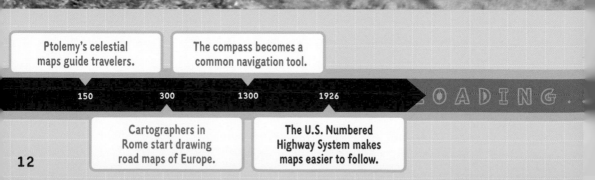

Ptolemy's celestial maps guide travelers.

The compass becomes a common navigation tool.

150   300   1300   1926

OADING

Cartographers in Rome start drawing road maps of Europe.

The U.S. Numbered Highway System makes maps easier to follow.

Road Signs

Over the next hundreds of years, Europeans explored the world. They settled in many new places. Cartographers were busy making maps of all the cities they found and built. In the United States, some roads were known by many names. So what name goes on the map? In 1926, U.S. highways got official numbers. Finally, the numbers on the road and the map matched.

Travel was easier with road signs. But wait—is that highway 4 the same as the highway 4 we just passed? In 1927, U.S. road signs got a set of rules. A manual was printed. Different types of roads have signs of a certain color or shape. U.S. Highway 4's sign is different than State Route 4's sign. Now drivers can be sure they are on the right road.

U.S. highway signs all have a crest shape like this Highway 66 sign.

Ptolemy's celestial maps guide travelers.	The compass becomes a common navigation tool.		A manual for U.S. road signs is printed.	
150	300	1300	1926	1927
	Cartographers in Rome start drawing road maps of Europe.		The U.S. Numbered Highway System makes maps easier to follow.	

LEFT
EXIT 1A

City Center
S Waterfront
↓ EXIT ONLY ↓

405
NORTH
To
Beavert

EXIT
↖ 1 A

| Ptolemy's celestial maps guide travelers. | The compass becomes a common navigation tool. | A manual for U.S. road signs is printed. |

150 300 1300 1926 1927 1971

| Cartographers in Rome start drawing road maps of Europe. | The U.S. Numbered Highway System makes maps easier to follow. | Mileposts and exit numbers are posted on interstates. |

Drivers got to know which road they were on. But sometimes it was tricky knowing exactly where they were. **Mileposts** and **exit** numbers soon became standard. By 1961, many states had these road markers. As of 1971, all **interstate highways** posted exit numbers. They are on the map, too. Now you won't miss that turn!

No matter which US city you visit, you will see standard highway signs like these.

Digital Maps

In 2000, maps started getting posted to the Internet. MapQuest was the first to offer online **digital maps**. Yahoo followed in 2004. In 2005, Google Maps joined them. People could print turn-by-turn directions between almost any two places. These are still popular apps. Today, people look up about a billion maps on Google each day!

A man uses a tablet to go online and find directions.

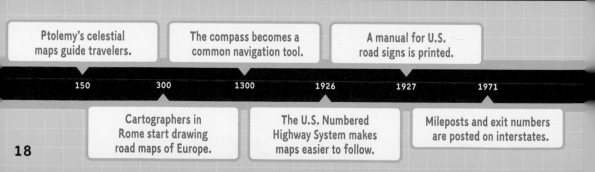

Ptolemy's celestial maps guide travelers.

The compass becomes a common navigation tool.

A manual for U.S. road signs is printed.

| 150 | 300 | 1300 | 1926 | 1927 | 1971 |

Cartographers in Rome start drawing road maps of Europe.

The U.S. Numbered Highway System makes maps easier to follow.

Mileposts and exit numbers are posted on interstates.

LOADING . . . LOADING . . .

The first digital
maps go online.

A driver can attach a TomTom receiver to the windshield to get directions on the go.

Ptolemy's celestial maps guide travelers.

The compass becomes a common navigation tool.

A manual for U.S. road signs is printed.

150 300 1300 1926 1927 1971

Cartographers in Rome start drawing road maps of Europe.

The U.S. Numbered Highway System makes maps easier to follow.

Mileposts and exit numbers are posted on interstates.

The U.S. military had been using a **Global Positioning System (GPS)** for their crafts for decades. They used satellites to see where they were and where they were going. In 2000, GPS became available for everyone. In 2004, the TomTom GO was the first handheld GPS receiver for drivers. Drivers could punch in an address. Then TomTom would speak directions while they drove!

The TomTom GO becomes the first in-car GPS of its kind.

2000   2004   ING... LOADING...

The first digital maps go online.

By 2007, people were using all sorts of digital maps. And people were carrying many kinds of cell phones. Then the Apple iPhone was released. It was one of the first phones with a GPS receiver and the Google Maps app. Now people had directions in the palms of their hands, inside and outside of their cars!

People can see where they are on their phones in real time—even on the train.

Ptolemy's celestial maps guide travelers.		The compass becomes a common navigation tool.		A manual for U.S. road signs is printed.	
150	300	1300	1926	1927	1971
	Cartographers in Rome start drawing road maps of Europe.		The U.S. Numbered Highway System makes maps easier to follow.		Mileposts and exit numbers are posted on interstates.

The TomTom GO becomes the
first in-car GPS of its kind.

2000   2004   2007   . . . L O A D I N G . . .

The first digital
maps go online.

Google Maps first appears
on the Apple iPhone.

Ptolemy's celestial
maps guide travelers.

The compass becomes a
common navigation tool.

A manual for U.S.
road signs is printed.

150   300   1300   1926   1927   1971

Cartographers in
Rome start drawing
road maps of Europe.

The U.S. Numbered
Highway System makes
maps easier to follow.

Mileposts and exit numbers
are posted on interstates.

How about directions on your wrist? In 2012, Garmin created a GPS watch just for outdoor adventurers. This watch tracks where you are. The internal compass points you which way to go. It tells you how long it will take to get there, too. As long as a satellite can find your watch, you'll never get lost.

GPS receivers have gotten small enough to fit in a watch. Hikers can carry maps on their wrists.

The TomTom GO becomes the first in-car GPS of its kind.

Garmin sells its first GPS wristwatch for hikers.

2000   2004   2007   2012   ADING...

The first digital maps go online.

Google Maps first appears on the Apple iPhone.

In only a few short years, people came to rely on GPS to find their way. Why not put it right in the dashboard? By 2016, built-in GPS became common in new cars. This system shows drivers the quickest route. Just like smartphone apps, car GPS systems warn drivers of traffic, accidents, and road construction.

A screen in the car's dash has a map. The red triangle shows where the car is.

Ptolemy's celestial maps guide travelers.

The compass becomes a common navigation tool.

A manual for U.S. road signs is printed.

150 300 1300 1926 1927 1971

Cartographers in Rome start drawing road maps of Europe.

The U.S. Numbered Highway System makes maps easier to follow.

Mileposts and exit numbers are posted on interstates.

The TomTom GO becomes the first in-car GPS of its kind.

Garmin sells its first GPS wristwatch for hikers.

2000   2004   2007   2012   2016

The first digital maps go online.

Google Maps first appears on the Apple iPhone.

Built-in GPS becomes more common in cars.

Ptolemy's celestial
maps guide travelers.

The compass becomes a
common navigation tool.

A manual for U.S.
road signs is printed.

150   300   1300   1926   1927   1971

Cartographers in
Rome start drawing
road maps of Europe.

The U.S. Numbered
Highway System makes
maps easier to follow.

Mileposts and exit numbers
are posted on interstates.

Into the Future!

You'll probably never have to navigate by the stars. You have a world of maps and directions at your fingertips. What could be better than that? How about a "map" that actually takes you where you want to go? This map is a driverless car. It uses GPS, **sensors**, and cameras to make a course and take you for a ride. Finding your way keeps getting easier!

Carmaker Volkswagen shows off an idea for a driverless car.

The TomTom GO becomes the first in-car GPS of its kind.	Garmin sells its first GPS wristwatch for hikers.	Driverless cars may become a navigation tool.

| 2000 | 2004 | 2007 | 2012 | 2016 | 2020s |

The first digital maps go online.	Google Maps first appears on the Apple iPhone.	Built-in GPS becomes more common in cars.

Glossary

astronomer A scientist who studies the sun, moon, and stars.

cartographer A person who makes maps.

celestial body An object in the sky outside the Earth, such as the sun, moon, stars, or planets.

compass An instrument for finding directions with a magnetic needle that always points north.

digital map A map created on a computer and designed to be used on screens.

exit A ramp or road off a major highway.

Global Positioning System (GPS) A system of satellites that orbit the Earth and send signals to GPS receivers in order to calculate the receiver's position.

interstate highway A main road with no stop lights designed to let people quickly drive across the country and through the states.

magnetic field A force that attracts metals; Earth has magnetic fields at the North and South poles.

milepost A road sign that marks each mile along a road.

navigate To plot a course and find your way while traveling.

sensor An instrument that reacts to changes in heat, sound, pressure, or movement.

smartphone A cell phone that acts like a computer and can connect to the Internet.

Read More

Linde, Barbara M. *All about Road Maps and GPS.* New York: Gareth Stevens Publishing, 2019.

Maurer, Tracy Nelson. *Using Road Maps and GPS.* Minneapolis, Minn.: Lerner Publications, 2017.

McAneney, Caitlin. *The Compass Rose and Cardinal Directions.* New York: Gareth Stevens Publishing, 2015.

Websites

ESA Kids Technology: Satellite Navigation
www.esa.int/esaKIDSen/SEMICLXJD1E_Technology_0.html

Kiddle: Navigation
https://kids.kiddle.co/Navigation

Kids Discover: Maps
www.kidsdiscover.com/shop/issues/maps-for-kids

Kids Geography: Usefulness of Maps
https://kidsgeo.com/geography-for-kids/usefulness-of-maps

Index

About the Author

Rachel Grack has worked in children's nonfiction publishing since 1999. Rachel lives on a small desert ranch in Arizona. She enjoys spending time with her family and barnyard of animals. Thanks to our wireless world, her ranch stays tapped into developing technology.

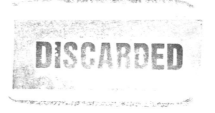